E COMMERCE SEO STRATEGIES

Selling Online Succesfully

Neil J Milliner

Books by Neil J Milliner

BOOKS BY
NEIL J MILLINER

CONTENTS

DISCLAIMER:

The publisher and the author make no guarantees concerning the level of success you may experience by following the advice and strategies contained in this book, and you accept the risk that results will differ for each individual. The testimonials and examples provided in this book show results which may not apply to the average reader and are not intended to represent or guarantee that you will achieve the same or similar results.

The publisher and the author do not make any guarantee or other promise as to any results that may be obtained from using the content of this book. You should never make any investment decision without first consulting with your own financial advisor and conducting your own research and due diligence. To the maximum extent permitted by law, the publisher and the author disclaim any and all liability in the event any information, commentary, analysis, opinions, advice and/or recommendations contained in this book prove to be inaccurate, incomplete or unreliable, or result in any investment or other losses.

E-COMMERCE SEO STRATEGIES

SELLING ONLINE SUCCESSFULLY

E-COMMERCE SEO STRATEGIES:
Selling Online Successfully
By Neil J Milliner

Chapter 1. Introduction to On-Site E-commerce SEO

Unleash Your E-commerce Sales Potential: A Quick Guide to On-Site SEO

In the bustling world of online shopping, where thousands of businesses vie for attention, visibility is everything. That's where on-site SEO comes in, your secret weapon for boosting your e-commerce store's ranking in search engine results and attracting more customers. Imagine this: when someone searches for "eco-friendly sneakers," your optimized product pages magically appear near the top, leading eager shoppers right to your door. On-site SEO makes this magic happen.

Think of your website as an inviting storefront. On-site SEO is like dressing it up with the right keywords, informative product descriptions, and a clear, easy-to-navigate layout. Search engines love this! They see your site as relevant, trustworthy, and user-friendly, rewarding you with higher rankings. This means more potential customers clicking through, browsing your products, and eventually hitting that "Buy Now" button.

On-site SEO isn't just about fancy tricks, though. It's about understanding your customers and giving them the experience they crave. Think high-quality product images, detailed descriptions that answer their questions, and a smooth checkout process. When you make things easy and informative, search engines take notice and your customers stay happy.

So, unlock the power of on-site SEO and watch your e-commerce store rise to the top. Remember, it's an investment that pays off in loyal customers, booming sales, and a thriving online presence. Are you ready to unleash your e-commerce magic?

Chapter 2. Understanding Keywords for E-commerce

E-commerce Visibility Gold Rush: Dig Deeper with Keywords

Forget panning for gold. The real riches in e-commerce lie buried in the treasure trove of relevant keywords. These hidden gems, once unearthed, illuminate your online store to eager shoppers, drawing them in like moths to a flame.
But navigating the keyword jungle can be tricky.

HERE'S YOUR MAP TO SUCCESS:

- Laser Focus: Instead of generic "running shoes," target niches with "women's minimalist trail running shoes." These long-tail beauties may have lower search volume, but they attract highly qualified leads – customers ready to buy exactly what you offer.
- Keyword Alchemy: Tools like Google Keyword Planner and SEMrush become your trusty prospector's pickaxe. Uncover hidden search trends, assess competition, and refine your list to strike gold with keywords that perfectly match your products and audience.
- Strategic Sprinkle: Don't just stuff keywords like a holiday turkey. Infuse them seamlessly into product descriptions, titles, and even blog posts. Think of them as spices, adding flavor without overpowering the dish. Remember, user experience is king!

Mastering the keyword dance lets your e-commerce store waltz to the top of search engine results, showcasing your wares to a captive audience. Forget panning for crumbs – this is a gold rush you won't want to miss!

Chapter 3. Optimizing Product Titles and Descriptions

Headline Grabbers: Crafting Product Titles That Captivate and Convert

Imagine your product title as the first impression your online storefront makes. It's the tiny billboard vying for attention in a crowded digital marketplace. So, how do you craft a title that's both irresistibly catchy and SEO-friendly, guiding customers to your doorstep like a shimmering oasis in the search engine desert?

SEO Savvy:

Think of keywords like secret spices. Sprinkle them strategically throughout your title, but remember, a delicious dish is all about balance. Aim for natural integration, avoiding keyword stuffing that reads like a robot wrote it. Tools like Google Keyword Planner and SEMrush can be your culinary companions, helping you discover the right ingredients and assess the competition's spice cabinet.

Clarity is King:

Confusing titles are like cryptic menus – they leave customers hungry for answers and frustratedly clicking away. Be clear and concise, highlighting your product's key features and benefits. Think of it as a short, attention-grabbing synopsis of your product's story.

Curiosity Catalyst:

A touch of intrigue can be the secret sauce that sets your title apart. Spark curiosity with a hint of mystery, a surprising benefit, or a clever play on words. Remember, a little sizzle can go a long way in luring customers in for a closer look.

Example Time:

Let's put theory into practice. Imagine you're selling a cozy, ultra-soft blanket. Instead of the generic

"Soft Blanket," consider these SEO-friendly and captivating options:

- "Snuggle Sanctuary: The Blanket That Hugs You Back" (appeals to emotion and uses a descriptive keyword)
- "Melt Your Stress Away: The Luxuriously Soft Blanket for Ultimate Relaxation" (highlights a key benefit and uses long-tail keywords)
- "Cuddly Cloud: Escape to Pure Comfort with This Heavenly Blanket" (uses evocative imagery and a playful metaphor)

Remember, these are just starting points! Experiment with different formats and tones to find what resonates with your target audience and aligns with your brand voice.

Beyond Titles:
Engaging product titles are just the first bite of the apple. To truly captivate customers, you need irresistibly delicious descriptions. Think of them as the detailed menu that brings your product to life, painting a picture of its benefits and features in vivid language.

Sensory Symphony:
Engage all five senses with your descriptions. Let customers imagine the warmth of your blanket against their skin, the soft sigh of relief as they sink into its comfort. Use descriptive adjectives and evocative verbs to paint a sensory portrait that draws them in.

Storytelling Magic:
Weave a narrative around your product. Tell the story of its creation, its unique features, or the joy it brings to users. People connect with stories, so make your product's story one they'll remember.

Benefits Before Features:
Don't just list features; highlight the benefits they offer. Instead of "Made from 100% organic cotton," say "Experience pure, breathable comfort with our organic cotton blanket." Focus on how your product improves customers' lives, not just its technical specs.

Call to Action:
Don't leave customers hanging! Include a clear call to action, like "Add to cart and snuggle up today!" or "Treat yourself to ultimate relaxation – order now!" Make it easy for them to take the next step and bring your product home.

Remember, crafting compelling product titles and descriptions is an art, not a science. Experiment, have fun, and let your creativity shine through. With a dash of SEO savvy and a sprinkle of storytelling magic, you'll create titles and descriptions that captivate customers, boost your search engine ranking, and ultimately, turn online browsers into loyal fans.

Bonus Tip:
Use high-quality product images that complement your titles and descriptions. Visuals can be powerful persuasion tools, so showcase your product in its best light!

I hope this helps you craft product titles and descriptions that are both irresistible and SEO-friendly. Good luck!

Chapter 4. Image Optimization for Better Visibility

1. Enhance your online visibility and boost product discoverability with our guide on optimizing product images for search engines. Explore the significance of fine-tuning your visuals to align with search engine algorithms, ensuring that your products stand out and attract the attention they deserve. Maximize the potential of image optimization to drive traffic, improve search rankings, and ultimately enhance the overall online presence of your products.

2. Unlock the power of SEO with our valuable tips on crafting image alt text that enhances your website's visibility. Learn the art of creating SEO-friendly alt text for images, ensuring they not only describe your visuals accurately but also contribute to improved search engine rankings. Explore effective strategies to optimize your website's accessibility and boost its overall performance in search results. Elevate your SEO game by mastering the creation of compelling and search-friendly alt text for images.

Chapter 5. Creating a User-Friendly URL Structure

1.Uncover the importance of maintaining a clean and organized URL structure as we delve into its impact on enhancing user experience and search engine optimization. Explore the key reasons why a structured URL can contribute to the overall success of your website and learn how to implement best practices for a streamlined online presence.

2. Elevate your website's user experience and SEO performance with our expert tips on crafting user-friendly and search engine optimized URLs. Dive into practical strategies for creating URLs that are not only easy for users to navigate but also align with SEO best practices, ensuring improved visibility and rankings. Master the art of designing URLs that contribute to a seamless browsing experience and enhance your website's overall accessibility.

Chapter 6. Implementing Structured Data Markup

1. Embark on a journey into the world of structured data with our comprehensive introduction, exploring its profound impact on shaping search results. Delve into the fundamental concepts of structured data and discover how it plays a pivotal role in influencing the way search engines interpret and present information. Uncover the potential benefits of incorporating structured data and gain insights into optimizing your content for enhanced visibility in search results.

2. Navigate the realm of e-commerce success by mastering the implementation of structured data. Unlock the secrets to leveraging structured data effectively for e-commerce websites, as we provide step-by-step guidance on enhancing your product listings. Learn the art of presenting information in a structured format that not only appeals to search engines but also elevates the visibility and performance of your e-commerce site. Maximize the impact of structured data to drive traffic, improve rankings, and boost conversions for your online store.

Chapter 7. Mobile Optimization for Enhanced User Experience

1. Explore the critical role of mobile optimization in elevating the success of e-commerce SEO with our insightful exploration. Understand why prioritizing mobile responsiveness is essential for capturing a wider audience and improving search engine rankings. Uncover the impact of mobile-friendly design on user experience and learn how it directly contributes to the overall success of your e-commerce endeavors.

2. Elevate your online presence and user engagement with our expert tips on creating a responsive and mobile-friendly website. Dive into practical strategies that ensure your website adapts seamlessly to various devices, offering an optimal viewing experience for users on smartphones and tablets. Learn how to enhance the responsiveness of your site, improve loading times, and implement design elements that cater to the growing mobile audience. Stay ahead in the digital landscape by mastering the art of crafting websites that are both visually appealing and functionally efficient on mobile devices.

Chapter 8. Internal Linking Strategies

1. Navigate the realm of e-commerce success by delving into the realm of effective internal linking practices with our comprehensive guide. Uncover the strategies and tactics that can transform your e-commerce site's internal linking structure, fostering improved navigation and user experience. Explore how strategic internal linking can enhance the discoverability of products, boost page authority, and contribute to the overall success of your online store.

2. Demystify the role of internal links in the realm of SEO with our in-depth exploration. Understand how internal linking serves as a cornerstone for search engine optimization and discover the ways in which it influences your website's visibility and rankings. Dive into the intricacies of link equity, content relevance, and user navigation, gaining valuable insights into how internal links can be harnessed to strengthen your site's SEO foundation. Master the art of strategic internal linking and unlock the full potential of your website in the digital landscape.

Chapter 9. Customer Reviews and Ratings

1. Unleash the power of customer reviews and ratings as we explore how to leverage them for significant SEO benefits. Dive into the impact of user-generated feedback on search engine rankings and discover strategies to incorporate customer testimonials effectively. Learn how genuine reviews can enhance the credibility of your online presence, boost trust among potential customers, and contribute to improved visibility in search results.

2. Empower your online community by discovering the art of encouraging user-generated content. Delve into effective strategies for motivating your audience to share their experiences, opinions, and insights. Explore the SEO advantages of user-generated content and learn how it can amplify your online presence. From customer testimonials to social media engagement, unlock the potential of user-generated content to not only enrich your brand narrative but also enhance your website's

visibility in search engine results.

Chapter 10. Site Speed and Its Impact on SEO

1. Gain insights into the intricate relationship between site speed and search rankings as we unravel the impact of loading times on your online visibility. Explore the critical connection between a fast-loading website and its influence on search engine rankings. Understand why site speed matters and how optimizing it can significantly enhance your website's performance in search results, ultimately attracting more visitors and improving user satisfaction.

2. Elevate your website's user experience and search engine performance with our expert tips on improving loading times. Dive into practical strategies for optimizing your website's speed, from image compression to efficient coding practices. Learn how a faster-loading site not only enhances user satisfaction but also positively influences search rankings. Master the art of balancing aesthetics and functionality to ensure your website loads swiftly, capturing the attention of both users and search engines alike.

Chapter 11. E-commerce SEO and Social Media Integration

1. Unleash the potential of social media to boost your visibility in search results as we delve into effective utilization strategies. Explore how a strong social media presence can positively impact your search rankings and overall online visibility. Understand the symbiotic relationship between social media and search engines, and discover how to leverage platforms like Facebook, Twitter, and Instagram to enhance your brand's discoverability in the digital landscape.

2. Elevate your SEO game by mastering the art of integrating social media into your digital strategy. Unlock a wealth of strategies that seamlessly blend social media efforts with search engine optimization. From optimizing social profiles to creating shareable content, explore actionable techniques that amplify your online presence. Learn how to harness the power of social signals to influence search rankings and engage a broader audience. Maximize the synergy between social media and SEO to establish a strong and influential online presence.

Chapter 12. Handling Out-of-Stock Products

1. Navigate the challenges of managing out-of-stock products with our guide to best practices for SEO. Explore effective strategies to handle inventory fluctuations while maintaining a positive impact on your search rankings. From clear communication to alternative recommendations, learn how to seamlessly manage out-of-stock products to enhance user experience and ensure that your website remains optimized for search engines.

2. Safeguard your search rankings by implementing proactive measures to prevent negative impacts caused by out-of-stock products. Delve into strategies that not only address product unavailability but also contribute to maintaining a favorable SEO standing. Discover the importance of proper communication, strategic redirects, and alternative recommendations to mitigate the potential drawbacks of out-of-stock situations. Elevate your e-commerce strategy by mastering the art of handling inventory fluctuations without compromising your website's search engine optimization.

Chapter 13. E-commerce SEO Analytics

1. Uncover the significance of tracking and analyzing SEO metrics for e-commerce success with our comprehensive guide. Explore the key performance indicators that can shape your online visibility and understand how data-driven insights contribute to effective decision-making. Learn why monitoring SEO metrics is crucial for staying ahead in the competitive digital landscape and optimizing your e-commerce strategy for sustained growth.

2. Elevate your SEO game with our curated list of recommended tools for monitoring performance. Dive into the world of analytics and discover tools that provide actionable insights into your website's search engine optimization. From keyword tracking to backlink analysis, explore the functionalities of these tools and learn how they can empower you to make informed decisions. Stay on top of your SEO efforts by leveraging the capabilities of these tools and maximizing the impact of your e-commerce initiatives.

Chapter 14. Staying Updated with SEO Trends

1. Embrace the dynamic nature of SEO as we delve into its ever-evolving landscape and the crucial importance of staying informed. Explore the rapid changes and updates that characterize the world of search engine optimization. Understand how continuous learning and awareness are integral to navigating the dynamic challenges of SEO, ensuring that your strategies remain effective and aligned with the latest industry standards.

2. Stay ahead in the ever-changing realm of SEO with our expert tips on keeping up with the latest trends. Dive into practical strategies for staying informed about algorithm updates, emerging techniques, and evolving best practices. From subscribing to industry publications to participating in forums and webinars, explore actionable methods to stay abreast of the dynamic SEO landscape. Empower yourself with the knowledge and insights needed to adapt your strategies and maintain a competitive edge in the ever-evolving world of search engine optimization.

Chapter 15. Conclusion

1. Unlock the essentials of on-site e-commerce SEO with our comprehensive summary of key points. Delve into the intricacies of optimizing your online store for search engines, covering crucial aspects such as meta tags, product descriptions, and internal linking. Gain a holistic understanding of on-site SEO practices that can significantly impact your e-commerce success, ensuring that your website is primed for improved visibility and user experience.

2. Embrace the continuous journey of successful SEO as we emphasize the ongoing effort required for sustained results. Recognize that SEO is not a one-time task but an evolving process that demands consistent attention and adaptation. Explore the dynamic nature of search engine algorithms and discover strategies to keep your website optimized for changing trends. From regular content updates to monitoring analytics, learn how persistent effort is key to achieving and maintaining success in the ever-competitive landscape of online visibility.

Chapter 16. FAQ

CHAPTER 1:

On-Site E-commerce SEO: Boosting Visibility and Sales

In the vibrant marketplace of e-commerce, visibility is everything. Your website, your carefully curated storefront, needs to shine brighter than the rest to attract customers and convert them into loyal fans. And the secret weapon to achieving this digital prominence? Mastering the art of on-site SEO.

This isn't a mere technical endeavor; it's a strategic symphony, where every note, from keywords to content and user experience, harmonizes to create a website that search engines adore and customers flock to. This chapter is your comprehensive guide to composing this symphony, unlocking actionable insights to enhance your website's performance and watch your sales soar.

UNVEILING THE SEO MASTERCLASS:

- Keyword Alchemy: We'll dive into the treasure trove of relevant keywords, the golden search terms your target audience craves. You'll learn how to identify them, then weave them seamlessly into your website's fabric, from product titles to captivating descriptions, making your online store sing to search engines.
- Content as the Conductor: Beyond product listings, we'll explore the power of crafting irresistible blog posts, guides, and reviews. This content won't just rank high; it will engage visitors, establish your brand as a trusted authority, and keep them coming back for more.
- Technical Tune-up: Page speed, mobile responsiveness, and internal linking – these aren't just technical jargon; they're the orchestra's instruments. We'll show you how to optimize them for a seamless user experience, pleasing both search engines and customers alike.
- Conversion Optimization: The Grand Finale: Attracting visitors is crucial, but converting them into loyal customers is the true crescendo. Discover clever tactics to streamline your checkout process, build trust with product reviews, and personalize the shopping experience, turning casual browsers into enthusiastic shoppers.
- Staying Ahead of the Curve: The SEO landscape is ever evolving, but fear not! We'll equip you with the tools and knowledge to stay informed and adapt your strategies to the latest trends and algorithm updates, ensuring your website dances to the SEO beat, no matter the tempo.

ACTIONABLE INSIGHTS, NOT EMPTY PROMISES:

This chapter isn't just about reading; it's about doing. We'll provide practical tips, checklists, and real-world examples to help you implement these strategies on your own website. No jargon, no fluff, just actionable notes for your SEO symphony.

THE ULTIMATE REWARD:

By mastering on-site e-commerce SEO, you'll unlock a powerful lever for growth. Imagine your website climbing the search engine ranks, attracting relevant traffic, and seamlessly converting visitors into paying customers. That's the power of SEO, and this chapter is your roadmap to achieving it.

Ready to take the stage and conduct your website to e-commerce success? Turn the page and let's delve into the specifics, empowering your online store to thrive in the digital spotlight!

This chapter serves as a strong introduction to the world of on-site e-commerce SEO, setting the stage for further exploration in subsequent chapters. Feel free to share specific areas you'd like to delve deeper into, and I'll be happy to tailor the subsequent chapters to your unique needs and website.

CHAPTER 2:

Introduction to On-Site E-commerce SEO: Unlocking the Gateway to Visibility and Sales

Imagine your online store, your meticulously curated haven of products, lost in the labyrinthine depths of the internet. Customers seeking exactly what you offer can't find you, leaving you with empty shelves and dwindling dreams. This is the harsh reality of an e-commerce website devoid of the magic touch of on-site SEO.

Fear not, aspiring merchants! On-site SEO is your hidden treasure map, guiding you through the intricate pathways of search engine visibility and unlocking the gateway to a bustling marketplace. It's not just about technical jargon; it's about understanding how search engines navigate the digital landscape and strategically aligning your website with their preferences.

In this introductory chapter, we'll peel back the layers of this transformative discipline, unveiling its potential to:

- Boost your website's ranking: Climb the SERP ladder, leaving your competitors in the dust. Imagine potential customers stumbling upon your storefront before they even realize they were looking for it!
- Attract the right audience: No more casting a net blindly. On-site SEO lets you laser-focus on the customers who actually want your products, saving you time and resources.
- Convert browsers into buyers: Optimize your pages to guide visitors seamlessly through the buying journey, transforming fleeting interest into tangible sales.
- Build brand authority: Establish yourself as a trusted voice in your niche, fostering customer loyalty and repeat business.

THIS CHAPTER SERVES AS YOUR COMPASS, OUTLINING THE KEY PILLARS OF ON-SITE SEO:

- Keyword mastery: Learn how to identify the golden search terms that resonate with your audience and weave them seamlessly into your website's fabric.
- Content as king (and queen): Go beyond product listings! Craft captivating content that engages visitors, ranks high, and establishes your brand as an expert.
- Technical tune-up: Page speed, mobile responsiveness, and internal linking – these aren't just technical buzzwords; they're the foundation of a user-friendly website that search engines and customers adore.
- Conversion optimization: Make every click count by streamlining your checkout process, building trust with customer reviews, and personalizing the shopping experience.

But this is just the beginning! In the chapters that follow, we'll delve deeper into each of these pillars, providing practical tips, actionable strategies, and real-world examples to empower you to transform your website into a magnet for customers and sales.

Are you ready to embark on this journey? Turn the page and let's unlock the magic of on-site SEO, together!

CHAPTER 3:

Understanding Keywords for E-commerce: Your Search Engine Compass

Imagine navigating a dense jungle without a map. The path to your destination seems elusive, shrouded in foliage and uncertainty. In the online jungle of e-commerce, keywords are your map, guiding potential customers to your products and propelling your website to the forefront of search engine results.

This chapter equips you with the tools to decipher the language of the digital world, understanding the vital role keywords play in attracting the right audience and boosting your sales.

UNVEILING THE POWER OF KEYWORDS:

Think of keywords like whispers carried on the wind, revealing what potential customers are seeking. By identifying the right keywords, you're essentially tuning your website to these whispers, ensuring your products appear when customers search for terms relevant to your offerings.

BEYOND THE ONE-WORD WONDERS:

While short, generic keywords like "shoes" or "clothing" might seem tempting, they're often crowded marketplaces, difficult to compete in. This is where long-tail keywords come into play – your secret weapon in the e-commerce arena.

Long-tail keywords are more specific phrases, like "women's comfortable walking shoes for wide feet" or "eco-friendly bamboo t-shirts." These pinpoint the exact needs and desires of your target audience, attracting highly qualified leads who are closer to the point of purchase.

BENEFITS OF LONG-TAIL KEYWORDS:

- Lower competition: Fewer websites vie for these specific searches, making it easier to rank higher and capture valuable traffic.
- Higher conversion rates: Customers using long-tail keywords are further along in the buying journey, having a clear idea of what they want. This translates to improved conversion rates and a higher return on your SEO investment.
- Enhanced relevance: By incorporating long-tail keywords into your website content, you demonstrate a deeper understanding of your audience's needs, building trust and brand authority.

MASTERING THE KEYWORD ART:

Identifying the right long-tail keywords requires research and strategy. Tools like Google Keyword Planner and Ahrefs can help you discover relevant searches, analyze their competition, and track their popularity. Remember, it's not about stuffing your website with keywords; it's about using them naturally and strategically throughout your content, titles, and product descriptions.

THE KEY TAKEAWAYS:

Keywords are the foundation of any successful e-commerce SEO strategy. By understanding the power of long-tail keywords and implementing them effectively, you can attract the right audience, boost your website's visibility, and watch your sales soar.

This chapter is just the beginning of your keyword journey. In the following chapters, we'll delve deeper into:

- Advanced keyword research techniques
- Integrating keywords into your website content
- Tracking and analyzing keyword performance

Remember, your keyword strategy is a dynamic process, evolving alongside your business and the ever-changing online landscape. By continuously learning and adapting, you can ensure your website stays relevant, visible, and at the top of your customers' minds.

Are you ready to become a keyword champion and unlock the full potential of your e-commerce website? Turn the page and let's embark on this exciting journey together!

CHAPTER 4:

Optimizing Product Titles and Descriptions: Painting Words that Convert

Imagine your online store as a bustling marketplace, filled with an array of products, each vying for attention. But amidst the cacophony, how do you make yours stand out? The answer lies in the art of crafting captivating product titles and descriptions – words that paint a picture, pique curiosity, and ultimately, convert browsers into buyers.

THIS CHAPTER DELVES INTO THE INTRICACIES OF THIS ARTISTIC ENDEAVOR, EMPOWERING YOU TO:

Hook 'em with the Title:

Your product title is like a headline, a first impression that can make or break the click. It needs to be concise, informative, and most importantly, attention-grabbing. Here's how to make it shine:

- Include relevant keywords: Don't be cryptic! Identify the search terms your target audience uses and weave them naturally into the title.
- Highlight unique features: What makes your product different? Showcase its special qualities, materials, or benefits to entice customers.
- Keep it concise: Aim for clarity over grandeur. Search engines favor shorter titles, and so do busy online shoppers.
- Sparkle with emotion: Spark curiosity or excitement with evocative language. A well-phrased title can go a long way!

UNVEILING THE STORY IN THE DESCRIPTION:

Think of your product description as a captivating story, one that draws customers in and paints a vivid picture of the benefits they'll experience. Here's how to weave a spell with words:

- Go beyond just features: Explain how your product solves a problem or enhances a lifestyle. Focus on the benefits, not just the technical specifications.
- Paint a picture with words: Use descriptive language that evokes emotions and sensory experiences. Make your customer imagine themselves using and enjoying your product.
- Structure for readability: Break up your text with bullet points, subheadings, and short paragraphs. This makes the information easier to digest and visually appealing.
- Embrace authenticity: Inject your brand voice and personality into the description. Show your passion for your products and connect with your audience on a human level.

KEYWORDS – THE INVISIBLE HELPERS:

While captivating copy is crucial, don't forget the silent partners: keywords. Strategically incorporate relevant keywords throughout your description, but with discretion. Avoid keyword stuffing; prioritize naturalness and readability.

THE PERFECT BALANCE:

Optimizing product titles and descriptions is about finding the perfect balance between engaging your audience and satisfying search engine algorithms. Remember, these words are not just for bots; they're for real people making buying decisions.

BEYOND THE CHAPTER:

This chapter is just a brushstroke on the canvas of effective product copywriting. In the following chapters, we'll explore:

- Advanced techniques for keyword integration
- Using storytelling and emotional triggers
- Writing in your brand voice
- A/B testing and optimizing your product copy

Remember, your words are powerful tools. By mastering the art of product title and description writing, you can transform your online store into a magnet for customers and sales. So, pick up your pen (or keyboard!), unleash your creativity, and paint a masterpiece of e-commerce copy that leaves customers wanting more!

CHAPTER 5:

Image Optimization for Better Visibility: Speaking Volumes Through Pixels

In the visual feast of e-commerce, captivating images aren't just window dressing; they're powerful tools for attraction, engagement, and ultimately, conversion. But the path to search engine visibility isn't just about eye-catching aesthetics; it demands strategic optimization that speaks volumes through pixels.

THIS CHAPTER UNVEILS THE SECRETS OF IMAGE OPTIMIZATION, EMPOWERING YOU TO:

Speed Up Your Website, Not Your Customers:

High-resolution images might be aesthetically pleasing, but they can weigh down your website like an anchor. Large file sizes translate to slow loading times, frustrating customers and sending them fleeing to faster competitors. Optimization comes to the rescue:

- Compress your images: Tools like TinyPNG and Photoshop can significantly reduce file size without sacrificing quality.
- Choose the right format: Opt for formats like JPEG for photos and PNG for graphics or images with transparency.
- Resize for digital screens: No one needs a desktop-sized image on their mobile phone. Resize images specifically for different screen sizes and devices.

KEYWORDS: THE BRIDGE BETWEEN IMAGE AND SEARCH ENGINE:

Just like with product titles and descriptions, keywords play a crucial role in image optimization. By incorporating relevant keywords into your image filenames and alt text, you're building a bridge between your visual content and search engine algorithms. Remember:

- Descriptive filenames: Instead of "IMG_1234.jpg," use informative names like "red-leather-wallet-for-men.jpg."
- Alt text is not just decoration: Write clear and concise alt text that describes the image content, using relevant keywords naturally.

MAKE IT ACCESSIBLE
FOR EVERYONE:

Accessibility isn't just about following guidelines; it's about inclusivity. Optimize your images with screen readers in mind:

- Descriptive alt text: Provide detailed descriptions that go beyond simple product names.
- Color contrast: Ensure enough contrast between text and background colors for those with visual impairments.
- Text overlays: For complex images, add text overlays summarizing the content.

BEYOND THE CHAPTER:

Image optimization is a continuous journey, not a one-time fix. In the following chapters, we'll delve deeper into:

- Advanced image compression techniques
- Utilizing image sitemaps for better indexing
- Leveraging visual search trends
- Testing and analyzing image performance

Remember, captivating images paired with strategic optimization are a winning combination. By mastering the art of speaking volumes through pixels, you can elevate your website's visibility, engage your audience, and watch your sales climb alongside your search engine ranking. So, grab your camera, fire up your editing software, and get ready to create visual masterpieces that not only delight your customers but also conquer the digital landscape!

CHAPTER 6:

Creating a User-Friendly URL Structure: Building a Navigational Compass

Imagine your website as a bustling bazaar, filled with an alluring array of products. But without a clear map, even the most eager shopper might get lost in the labyrinthine alleys. In the digital world, your URL structure serves as that map, guiding both users and search engines through the intricate pathways of your website. It's not just about technical mumbo jumbo; it's about crafting a clear, intuitive system that enhances user experience and boosts your SEO performance.

This chapter equips you with the tools to build a user-friendly URL structure, one that empowers both humans and algorithms to navigate your website with ease.

CLARITY BEFORE CLICKS:

A good URL should tell users where they are and what they'll find before they even click. This means avoiding cryptic, generic names like "page1.html" or "productX.php." Instead, strive for:

- Descriptive phrases: Use relevant keywords that accurately reflect the page content. Think "blue-cotton-t-shirt" instead of "clothing-item-123."
- Short and sweet: Keep your URLs concise and easy to remember. No one wants to wrestle with a URL longer than a dragon's tongue.
- Consistency is key: Maintain a consistent structure throughout your website. Whether it's "/category/product_name" or "/brand/product_name," choose a system and stick to it.

SEO'S SILENT ALLY:

A user-friendly URL structure isn't just about human convenience; it's also a secret weapon for SEO. Search engines favor websites with clear, organized URLs, making them easier to crawl and index. This translates to:

- Improved keyword ranking: Relevant keywords embedded in your URLs can signal to search engines what your page is about, potentially boosting your visibility for those specific terms.
- Enhanced crawlability: A logical structure helps search engine bots understand the relationships between pages on your website, improving indexing and discoverability.
- User signals: A user navigating your website through clear URLs sends positive signals to search engines, indicating relevance and trustworthiness.

BUILDING YOUR NAVIGATIONAL COMPASS:

Here are some practical tips for crafting user-friendly and SEO-friendly URL structures:

- Start with your categories: Identify your main categories and subcategories, building a hierarchical structure like "/clothing/shoes/sneakers."
- Use hyphens, not underscores: Hyphens separate words more naturally for both humans and search engines.
- Avoid special characters and numbers: Stick to letters, numbers, and hyphens for clean and crawlable URLs.
- Use lowercase characters: Consistent lowercase formatting improves readability and avoids potential indexing issues.

BEYOND THE CHAPTER:

Creating a user-friendly URL structure is just one step in your SEO journey. In the following chapters, we'll explore:

- Internal linking strategies for enhanced navigation
- Mobile-friendliness and URL optimization
- Tracking and analyzing website traffic through URLs
- Best practices for managing URL changes and redirects

Remember, your URL structure is not just a technical detail; it's a fundamental aspect of user experience and search engine optimization. By investing time and effort in crafting a clear and organized system, you'll empower your website to attract, engage, and convert visitors, transforming your digital bazaar into a haven for both customers and search engines. So, pick up your navigational compass, chart a course through the URL jungle, and watch your website blossom under the spotlight of online visibility!

CHAPTER 7:

Implementing Structured Data Markup: Speaking
the Language of Search Engines

Imagine you're having a conversation with someone who only understands one-word cues. It's frustrating, right? That's how search engines experience your website if it lacks structured data markup – they simply see a jumble of text and images, missing the valuable context that could boost your visibility and attract the right customers.

THIS CHAPTER BREAKS DOWN THE MYSTERY OF STRUCTURED DATA MARKUP, EMPOWERING YOU TO:

Unlock the Treasure of Context:

Structured data markup is like a translator, transforming the information on your website into a language search engines can understand. It provides them with detailed context about your products, reviews, prices, and other crucial elements, allowing them to display richer and more informative snippets in search results.

BENEFITS BEYOND VISIBILITY:

While improved search ranking is a major benefit, structured data markup offers more:

- Enhanced click-through rates: Rich snippets, including star ratings or price information, entice users to click, boosting your website traffic.
- Increased user engagement: Users can see key details directly in search results, improving their understanding and reducing bounce rates.
- Voice search optimization: Structured data plays a crucial role in voice search results, making your website discoverable when customers ask questions via voice assistants.

CHOOSING THE RIGHT SCHEMA:

Think of schemas as different dialects of the structured data language. Each schema is designed for specific types of content, like products, reviews, events, or recipes. Choose the schema that best represents the information you want to mark up – there are hundreds available!

IMPLEMENTATION: THE MANY PATHS:

There are several ways to implement structured data markup:

- Directly in your website code: Skilled developers can edit your website's HTML to include the markup directly.
- CMS plugins and extensions: Many content management systems offer plugins that simplify the process of adding structured data.
- Data Highlighter tool: Google's Data Highlighter tool lets you visually select elements on your webpage and associate them with the relevant schema.

TESTING AND VERIFICATION:

Once implemented, use Google's Structured Data Testing Tool to validate your markup and ensure it's error-free. This ensures search engines can properly understand and utilize your data.

BEYOND THE CHAPTER:

Structured data markup is a powerful tool, but it's just one piece of the SEO puzzle. In the following chapters, we'll explore:

- Advanced strategies for schema implementation
- Integrating structured data with Google Search Console
- Using structured data for local SEO
- Tracking and analyzing the impact of structured data on your website performance

Remember, by speaking the language of search engines through structured data markup, you unlock a hidden world of improved visibility, deeper customer engagement, and ultimately, greater success for your e-commerce website. So, pick your schema, choose your implementation method, and start translating your content into a language that attracts both users and search engines. Watch your website climb the rankings and thrive in the digital marketplace!

CHAPTER 8:

Mobile Optimization: Unlocking the Keys to the Micro Kingdom

Imagine your e-commerce website as a bustling marketplace, its shelves laden with treasures just waiting to be discovered. But what if most of your potential customers can only experience it through a narrow keyhole, missing out on the full richness and beauty? That's the harsh reality for websites not optimized for mobile devices, where the majority of online shopping now happens. In this digital landscape, mobile optimization is no longer a luxury; it's the key to unlocking the micro kingdom of millions of potential customers.

THIS CHAPTER EQUIPS YOU WITH THE TOOLS AND INSIGHTS TO:

Understand the Mobile Mandate:

Today, over 60% of all web traffic comes from mobile devices. Ignoring this massive audience is like closing your doors to the majority of potential customers. Mobile optimization isn't just about aesthetics; it's about ensuring a seamless and enjoyable shopping experience on all screen sizes.

SEO AND THE MOBILE IMPERATIVE:

Search engines prioritize mobile-friendly websites, boosting their visibility in search results. This means neglecting mobile optimization isn't just about losing customers; it's about losing crucial ground in the competitive online realm.

BEYOND JUST SHRINKING THINGS:

Mobile optimization goes beyond simply shrinking your desktop website onto a smaller screen. It's about:

- Responsive design: Choose a design that automatically adapts to different screen sizes and resolutions, ensuring optimal viewing on any device.
- Fast loading times: Mobile users are impatient. Optimize your images, code, and website structure to ensure lightning-fast loading times.
- Touch-friendly interface: Make sure buttons, menus, and forms are large enough and spaced for easy navigation with fingers.
- Prioritize content: Focus on showcasing the most important information first, optimizing product listings and calls to action for mobile screens.

ACTIONABLE TIPS FOR MOBILE MASTERY:

Here are some practical steps to optimize your e-commerce website for mobile devices:

- Test your website: Use Google's Mobile-Friendly Test tool to see how your website performs on mobile devices.
- Identify and fix issues: Address any errors or usability problems highlighted by the testing tool.
- Optimize your images: Compress images without sacrificing quality for faster loading times.
- Simplify your navigation: Avoid complex menus and focus on a clear and concise navigation structure.
- Utilize progressive web apps (PWAs): Consider implementing PWAs for an app-like experience on mobile devices, boosting engagement and conversions.

BEYOND THE CHAPTER:

Mobile optimization is a continuous journey, not a one-time fix. In the following chapters, we'll delve deeper into:

- Advanced responsive design techniques
- Mobile SEO best practices
- Leveraging mobile analytics to track user behavior
- A/B testing and optimizing your mobile experience

Remember, unlocking the micro kingdom of mobile users empowers your e-commerce website to reach new heights of visibility, engagement, and sales. Invest in mobile optimization, embrace the ever-evolving mobile landscape, and watch your digital marketplace flourish in the palm of your customers' hands!

CHAPTER 9:

Weaving a Web of Success: Internal Linking Strategies for E-commerce SEO

Imagine your e-commerce website as a sprawling labyrinth, filled with hidden treasures and enticing products. But without a map, even the most eager shopper might get lost in its winding corridors. Internal linking becomes your navigational compass, weaving a web of connections that guide users seamlessly through your virtual aisles and signal to search engines the true value of your content.

THIS CHAPTER UNLOCKS THE SECRETS OF STRATEGIC INTERNAL LINKING, EMPOWERING YOU TO:

Navigating the Labyrinth:

Internal links act as signposts, directing users from one page to another within your website. This not only enhances user experience by offering relevant information and keeping them engaged, but also strengthens your overall SEO by:

- Distributing Page Authority: Each page on your website has a certain "authority" in the eyes of search engines. Linking from high-authority pages (like popular product listings or informative blog posts) to other pages helps distribute this authority, boosting their ranking potential.
- Improving Crawlability: Search engine bots crawl your website through links, discovering and indexing hidden corners that might otherwise be missed. An efficient internal linking structure ensures bots can thoroughly explore your online labyrinth, leaving no treasure undiscovered.
- Relevancy Signals: By strategically linking related content, you signal to search engines the thematic connections between your pages. This helps them understand the overall structure and relevance of your website, potentially improving ranking for specific keywords.

FROM STRATEGY TO STRUCTURE:

Not all internal links are created equal. Here are some tips for weaving a web of success:

- Contextual Connections: Don't just stuff keywords into your links; focus on naturally integrating them into the context of your content. Think of each link as a helpful bridge leading users to further information.
- Anchor Text Matters: The text used in your link (anchor text) should be descriptive and relevant to the target page. Avoid generic terms like "click here" and opt for clear keywords or summaries of the landing page's content.
- Prioritize Deep Linking: While linking to popular product pages is important, don't neglect deeper content like blog posts or informational pages. Linking to these helps distribute page authority and provides search engines with a more comprehensive understanding of your website's value.
- Variety is Key: Don't just link from the same places all the time. Spread the link love across different parts of your website, ensuring all pages have a chance to shine in the spotlight.

TOOLS FOR YOUR WEAVING JOURNEY:

Several tools can help you analyze and optimize your internal linking structure:

- Google Search Console: This tool provides insights into your website's internal linking and highlights potential areas for improvement.
- Screaming Frog: This powerful tool crawls your website and generates detailed reports on internal links, broken links, and anchor text usage.
- SEMrush: This comprehensive SEO tool, among other features, offers internal linking analysis and suggestions for improving your overall linking strategy.

BEYOND THE CHAPTER:

Internal linking is just one thread in the complex tapestry of e-commerce SEO. In the upcoming chapters, we'll explore:

- Advanced techniques for keyword-rich anchor text
- Leveraging internal linking for specific SEO goals
- Tracking and analyzing the impact of internal linking
- Managing and maintaining your internal linking structure

Remember, by crafting a strategic and user-friendly internal linking web, you unlock the full potential of your e-commerce website. You connect users with relevant information, guide search engines to your hidden treasures, and ultimately, pave the way for a thriving online empire. So, pick up your needle and thread, unleash your inner weaver, and start crafting a web of success that leads to higher rankings, higher engagement, and higher sales!

CHAPTER 10:

The Golden Voices: Leveraging Customer Reviews and Ratings for E-commerce SEO

Imagine your online store as a bustling marketplace, its shelves bursting with products vying for attention. But amidst the cacophony, what makes customers stop and listen? In the digital world, the whispers of genuine customer reviews and the sparkle of star ratings hold the power to attract, engage, and ultimately, convert browsers into buyers.

This chapter unlocks the secrets of leveraging these golden voices to boost your e-commerce SEO and transform your virtual marketplace into a haven of trust and success.

THE POWER OF SOCIAL PROOF:

Customer reviews and ratings are more than just testimonials; they're social proof, the validation that potential buyers crave. Seeing positive reviews and high ratings reassures hesitant shoppers, builds trust in your brand, and ultimately influences their buying decisions.

SEO'S GOLDEN NUGGETS:

Reviews and ratings aren't just whispers; they're loud signals to search engines. Positive reviews and high ratings can:

- Improve search ranking: Search engines consider user-generated content a strong indicator of website relevance and trustworthiness, potentially boosting your search ranking for valuable keywords.
- Enrich search results: Google now displays star ratings and snippets of reviews directly in search results, making your listings stand out and attract more clicks.
- Enhance click-through rates: Positive reviews and star ratings entice users to click through to your website, increasing your traffic and potential sales.

CULTIVATING THE
REVIEW GARDEN:

Encouraging and managing customer reviews is an art. Here are some tips to cultivate a thriving garden of golden voices:

- Make it easy: Provide convenient and accessible ways for customers to leave reviews, like embedded forms or post-purchase emails.
- Incentivize participation: Offer discounts, loyalty points, or even entry into contests for leaving reviews, sparking customer engagement.
- Respond to every review: Both positive and negative reviews deserve your attention. Thankful responses solidify trust, while addressing negative feedback shows you care about customer satisfaction.
- Showcase your best: Feature positive reviews and high ratings prominently on your website and product pages, leveraging the power of social proof.

BEYOND THE CHAPTER:

Customer reviews and ratings are invaluable, but they're just one piece of the e-commerce SEO puzzle. In the following chapters, we'll explore:

- Advanced strategies for generating and managing online reviews
- Using review analytics to gain valuable customer insights
- Integrating reviews with social media marketing
- Addressing fake reviews and maintaining authenticity

Remember, your customers hold the microphones, and their voices hold immense power. By cultivating a thriving garden of genuine reviews and ratings, you'll not only build trust and boost your SEO, but also gain valuable insights and feedback to continuously improve your e-commerce offering. So, open your ears to the golden voices, nurture their expression, and watch your virtual marketplace blossom under the spotlight of authentic customer love!

CHAPTER 11:

The Need for Speed: Optimizing Your Website for SEO and Lightning-Fast Loading

Imagine navigating a bustling online marketplace, eager to explore its treasures. But with every click, you're met with agonizing delays, spinning loading bars, and the soul-crushing frustration of a sluggish website. In the digital world, speed is king, and a slow website is like a locked door to potential customers and search engine bots alike. This chapter delves into the crucial relationship between site speed and SEO, empowering you to unlock the doors to a streamlined shopping experience and climb the ranks of search results.

SPEED MATTERS MORE THAN EVER:

In today's fast-paced online world, patience is a rare commodity. Users expect websites to load instantly, and even a few seconds of delay can send them fleeing to a competitor. This isn't just about user experience; it's about SEO. Search engines like Google prioritize websites that offer lightning-fast loading times, deeming them more user-friendly and relevant.

The SEO Impact of Speedy Sites:

- Improved Ranking: Faster loading times can directly boost your search ranking, propelling your website closer to the top of search results where potential customers are most likely to click.
- Lower Bounce Rates: Speedy loading times ensure visitors don't abandon your website before they even begin exploring. This reduces bounce rates, a key metric that search engines consider when ranking websites.
- Enhanced Engagement: A streamlined website keeps users engaged, allowing them to browse products, interact with content, and ultimately convert into paying customers.

UNLOCKING THE SPEED TRAP:

But how do you achieve this elusive website speed? Here are some practical tips:

- Optimize your images: Large image files are major speed roadblocks. Compress images without sacrificing quality and resize them for web viewing.
- Leverage caching: Caching stores static content like images and HTML files, allowing them to load faster for returning visitors.
- Choose a reliable hosting provider: Invest in a quality hosting provider with robust infrastructure and fast server response times.
- Minimize HTTP requests: Every element on your website, from images to scripts, generates an HTTP request. Minimize unnecessary elements and prioritize efficient coding to reduce requests.
- Utilize Content Delivery Networks (CDNs): CDNs distribute your website content across geographically dispersed servers, ensuring faster loading times for users around the world.

TOOLS FOR MONITORING AND IMPROVEMENT:

Several tools can help you assess your website speed and identify areas for improvement:

- Google PageSpeed Insights: This free tool analyzes your website and provides actionable recommendations for improving speed.
- GTmetrix: This comprehensive tool offers detailed reports on your website's loading times and identifies potential bottlenecks.
- Pingdom Website Speed Test: This tool measures your website's loading time from different geographic locations, providing valuable insights into global performance.

BEYOND THE CHAPTER:

Site speed optimization is an ongoing journey, not a one-time fix. In the following chapters, we'll explore:

- Advanced techniques for image and code optimization
- Leveraging browser caching for further speed boosts
- Mobile-first speed optimization strategies
- Monitoring and tracking website speed performance over time

Remember, a fast website is not just a perk; it's a fundamental pillar of e-commerce success. By prioritizing speed, you'll not only improve user experience and conversions, but also climb the ranks of search results and unlock the full potential of your online marketplace. So, ignite your engines, implement these tips, and watch your website become a streamlined haven for happy customers and soaring SEO!

CHAPTER 12:

Weaving the Web: E-commerce SEO and Social Media Integration

Think of your e-commerce website as a magnificent castle, towering over the digital landscape. But standing alone, its grandeur might go unnoticed. Enter social media, a bustling market square teeming with potential customers. Through strategic integration, these two worlds can intertwine, transforming your castle into a beacon of visibility and attracting a throng of loyal visitors. This chapter delves into the powerful synergy between e-commerce SEO and social media, empowering you to weave a web that amplifies your online presence and drives success.

THE POWER OF SYNERGY:

Combining e-commerce SEO and social media is like fusing two powerful engines. Each fuels the other, creating a web of benefits:

- Enhanced Reach: Social media platforms offer immense reach, connecting you with potential customers beyond the scope of search engines. Sharing optimized content and product listings expands your audience and drives traffic back to your website, boosting SEO.
- Brand Building: Social media fosters meaningful connections with your customers. Engaging content and authentic interactions personalize your brand, build trust, and encourage user-generated content like reviews and shares, further strengthening your SEO profile.
- Keyword Amplification: Utilize social media to strategically incorporate relevant keywords in your posts and interactions. This strengthens your keyword presence beyond your website, sending positive signals to search engines and improving your ranking for those valuable terms.
- Content Expansion: Social media platforms open doors for diverse content beyond typical product pages. Share blog posts, infographics, user-generated content, and engaging videos. This variety attracts different audiences, extends your SEO reach, and keeps your brand fresh in users' minds.

WEAVING THE THREADS:

Here are some practical tips for integrating social media and e-commerce SEO:

- Optimize your social profiles: Include relevant keywords in your profile descriptions and bios to enhance discoverability through search.
- Share SEO-optimized content: Promote blog posts, product listings, and other website content on social media, adding clear calls to action to drive traffic back to your website.
- Utilize relevant hashtags: Research and strategically use hashtags related to your industry and products to increase your reach and attract targeted audiences.
- Run social media campaigns: Engage in targeted ad campaigns on social media platforms to promote specific products or deals, further amplifying your reach and visibility.
- Encourage user engagement: Respond to comments, answer questions, and participate in conversations on social media. This builds trust, generates user-generated content, and keeps your brand top-of-mind.
- Track and analyze your results: Use social media analytics tools to understand what works and what doesn't. Monitor engagement, clicks, and traffic generated to refine your strategy and maximize your SEO impact.

BEYOND THE CHAPTER:

The integration of e-commerce SEO and social media is an ongoing dance, not a static formula. In the following chapters, we'll explore:

- Advanced strategies for utilizing social media influencers
- Leveraging live video and interactive content for SEO benefits
- Analyzing and optimizing your social media content for maximum reach
- Integrating social media analytics with your overall SEO strategy

Remember, your website and social media are not isolated islands; they're interwoven threads in a tapestry of online success. By embracing the power of their synergy, you can weave a web of visibility, engagement, and ultimately, e-commerce triumph. So, pick up your needles, thread your social posts with optimized content, and watch your castle attract a kingdom of loyal customers under the ever-growing spotlight of search engine favor!

CHAPTER 13:

Facing the Empty Shelves: Strategies for Managing Out-of-Stock Products in E-commerce SEO

The bustling market square of your e-commerce website thrives on abundance. Products line the virtual shelves, enticing customers with their colorful displays and tempting descriptions. But what happens when those shelves fall empty, exposing the dreaded "Out of Stock" sign? The fear of plummeting SEO and frustrated customers can loom large. However, with strategic management, even empty shelves can be navigated, minimizing negative impacts and paving the way for future sales.

THE SEO DILEMMA:

Out-of-stock products present a two-pronged SEO challenge:

- Reduced Visibility: Search engines prioritize active products in their results. Inactive or out-of-stock listings can lose rankings and disappear from relevant searches, diminishing your overall website visibility.
- User Experience Disruption: Landing on an out-of-stock product page can be a frustrating experience, leading to increased bounce rates and potentially harming your website's trust with search engines.

FILLING THE VOID:

There's no magic spell to conjure instant inventory, but proactive strategies can mitigate the SEO woes of out-of-stock products:

- Transparency is Key: Clearly mark products as "Out of Stock" immediately. Don't let users waste time clicking through only to discover disappointment.
- Set Estimated Re-stock Dates: If possible, provide realistic timeframes for when the product will be back in stock. This keeps customers informed and potentially encourages them to wait or pre-order.
- Highlight Similar Products: Recommend alternative or similar products within the same category that are in stock. This helps retain user engagement and potentially leads to additional sales.
- Embrace Pre-Orders: For highly anticipated products, offer pre-order options. This creates excitement, gathers valuable customer data, and potentially boosts SEO by signaling pre-launch interest.
- Update Product Pages: Don't leave out-of-stock pages stagnant. Use the time to update your product descriptions, optimize keywords, and enhance visuals to keep them relevant for future searches.
- Leverage Internal Linking: Link out-of-stock pages to relevant active product listings or informational content within your website. This maintains internal link structure and keeps users engaged while the desired item is unavailable.

BEYOND THE CHAPTER:

Managing out-of-stock products requires ongoing vigilance and flexibility. In the following chapters, we'll explore:

- Advanced inventory management techniques to minimize out-of-stock situations
- Utilizing email marketing to notify customers about restocks and pre-order opportunities
- Monitoring user behavior and feedback on out-of-stock items to inform future product strategies
- Integrating out-of-stock product management with your overall SEO strategy

Remember, empty shelves are temporary setbacks, not permanent roadblocks. By implementing these strategies and remaining committed to user experience and SEO best practices, you can navigate the challenges of out-of-stock products with grace and resilience, ensuring your e-commerce market square remains a bustling hub of customer satisfaction and thriving online visibility. So, face the empty shelves with confidence, fill them with strategic solutions, and watch your website continue to attract customers and climb the ranks of search engine favor!

CHAPTER 14:

Tracking the Compass: E-commerce SEO Analytics for Ongoing Success

Imagine steering your e-commerce website through a vast digital ocean, navigating towards the vibrant island of success. Just like any seafaring voyager, you need a trusty compass – in this case, a comprehensive set of SEO analytics. By monitoring these vital metrics, you can chart your course, identify potential dangers, and adjust your sail to reach your SEO goals. This chapter unlocks the treasure chest of e-commerce SEO analytics, empowering you to gain valuable insights and steer your website towards ultimate search engine dominance.

THE LIGHTHOUSE OF VISIBILITY:

SEO metrics are the beacons that guide your way. Here are some
key metrics to monitor for e-commerce SEO success:

- Organic Traffic: The lifeblood of SEO, organic traffic measures the number of visitors who find your website through search engines without paid advertising. A steady increase in organic traffic indicates your SEO efforts are bearing fruit.
- Keyword Rankings: Track the ranking of your target keywords in search engine results pages (SERPs). This helps you understand how visible your website is for specific terms and identify areas for improvement.
- Conversion Rate: Ultimately, SEO success translates to sales. Monitor your conversion rate – the percentage of website visitors who complete a desired action (like making a purchase) – to assess the effectiveness of your SEO efforts in driving conversions.
- Bounce Rate: This metric reveals the percentage of users who leave your website after visiting just one page. A high bounce rate may indicate poor user experience or irrelevant content, demanding your attention and optimization.
- Backlinks: Think of backlinks as votes of confidence from other websites. The more high-quality backlinks you have, the more authority your website holds in the eyes of search engines, potentially boosting your rankings.
- Website Speed: Remember, users and search engines crave speed. Monitor your website loading times and address any bottlenecks to ensure a seamless experience and potentially improve your SEO performance.

UNVEILING THE HIDDEN TREASURES:

SEO analytics tools are your map and compass in one.
Here are some of the best for e-commerce:

- Google Search Console: This free tool by Google provides essential insights into your website's organic traffic, keyword rankings, and indexation status.
- SEMrush: This comprehensive platform offers in-depth SEO analysis, competitor research, keyword research, and backlink tracking, empowering you to craft an effective SEO strategy.
- Ahrefs: Another powerful tool, Ahrefs delves deep into backlinks, competitor analysis, and keyword research, offering valuable insights for improving your website's ranking potential.
- Google Analytics: This robust platform goes beyond SEO, providing detailed insights into user behavior, traffic sources, and conversions, helping you optimize your website for overall success.

BEYOND THE CHAPTER:

SEO analytics is not a one-time treasure hunt; it's an ongoing journey of discovery and refinement. In the following chapters, we'll explore:

- Advanced techniques for analyzing and interpreting SEO data
- Identifying and prioritizing areas for SEO improvement based on analytics
- Setting realistic SEO goals and tracking progress over time
- Integrating SEO analytics with other marketing channels for a holistic approach

Remember, your SEO data is a hidden treasure map, revealing valuable insights to steer your e-commerce website towards the island of success. By carefully monitoring key metrics, leveraging powerful tools, and continuously analyzing your data, you can adjust your sails, navigate SEO challenges with confidence, and watch your website rise to the top of the search engine horizon. So, grab your compass, set your course, and chart your path to ultimate online visibility!

CHAPTER 15:

Chasing the Horizon: Staying Ahead with SEO Trends

Imagine navigating your e-commerce website through a vast digital ocean, but the map you're using is outdated. The currents have shifted, new islands have emerged, and the winds of search engine algorithms have changed direction. In the ever-evolving landscape of SEO, staying informed about the latest trends is not just beneficial, it's essential for keeping your website afloat and reaching the island of search engine dominance. This chapter equips you with the tools and insights to become a master navigator of the SEO seas, always aware of the horizon and ready to adjust your sails to reach your goals.

WHY TRENDS MATTER:

The world of SEO is not static. Search engines constantly refine their algorithms, user behavior evolves, and new technologies emerge. Ignoring these trends is like setting your sails with blinders on, potentially leaving you adrift and watching your competitors surge ahead. Embracing the latest trends, however, allows you to:

- Optimize for Voice Search: As voice assistants become increasingly popular, understanding voice search trends and optimizing your content accordingly ensures you're heard loud and clear by the digital ear.
- Leverage Emerging Content Formats: Video, podcasts, and interactive content are gaining traction. Staying ahead of the curve in these formats can expand your reach and engage users in new ways.
- Embrace Evolving Local SEO: Local search is a powerhouse. Understanding the latest localized trends, like mobile-first indexing and hyper-local content strategies, can make your website an irresistible landmark for nearby customers.
- Utilize New Analytics Tools: New insights require new tools. Staying informed about the latest SEO analytics platforms and utilizing them effectively can reveal hidden treasures in your data, propelling you towards smarter optimization decisions.
- Keep Your Content Fresh: Google loves fresh content. By anticipating upcoming trends and tailoring your content accordingly, you can ensure your website stays relevant and exciting for both users and search engines.

NAVIGATING THE TREND CURRENTS:

So, how do you stay afloat in this dynamic ocean of SEO trends? Here are your trusty tools:

- Industry Publications and Blogs: Follow reputable SEO publications and blogs to stay updated on the latest news, insights, and case studies. Some industry giants include Search Engine Journal, Moz, and Search Engine Land.
- Conferences and Webinars: Attend industry conferences and webinars to learn from expert speakers, network with other professionals, and get firsthand exposure to emerging trends.
- Social Media Communities: Join active SEO communities on Twitter, LinkedIn, and Facebook. These platforms offer real-time discussions, Q&A sessions, and valuable peer-to-peer learning opportunities.
- Search Engine Announcements: Keep an eye on official announcements from Google and other search engines. They regularly shed light on upcoming algorithm changes and prioritize new ranking factors, giving you invaluable forewarning.
- Experimentation and Analysis: Don't be afraid to experiment with new trends in a controlled environment. Analyze the results, track your progress, and adapt your strategy based on what works and what doesn't.

BEYOND THE CHAPTER:

Staying ahead of the SEO curve is not a one-time voyage; it's a continuous journey of exploration and adaptation. In the following chapters, we'll delve deeper into:

- Advanced techniques for identifying and evaluating potential SEO trends
- Developing a flexible SEO strategy that can adapt to changing trends
- Integrating trend awareness with other aspects of your e-commerce marketing plan
- Measuring the impact of new trends on your website's SEO performance

Remember, the digital ocean of SEO is filled with exciting currents and uncharted territories. By embracing the latest trends, utilizing the right tools, and maintaining a spirit of exploration, you can navigate the ever-changing landscape with confidence, leaving your competitors in your wake and ultimately arriving at the island of online success. So, set your sails, embrace the horizon, and chase the waves of innovation – your e-commerce website's triumphant voyage awaits!

CONCLUSION:

The E-commerce SEO Odyssey - Weaving a Web of Visibility and Success

Congratulations! You've traversed the vibrant tapestry of this e-commerce SEO guide, navigating through chapters brimming with insights and strategies. We've explored the labyrinthine corridors of keyword research, unraveled the mysteries of technical optimization, and scaled the peaks of user experience. Now, standing at the conclusion of this digital odyssey, it's time to weave the threads of these chapters into a vibrant tapestry of your own e-commerce success.

Remember, SEO is not a linear path, but an ever-evolving landscape. The chapters you've encountered are not mere checkpoints, but stepping stones on a continual journey towards visibility and conversions. Let's revisit some of the crucial threads we've woven:

KEYWORDS: THE GOLDEN THREADS:

They are the anchors that hold your website in the churning sea of search results. Master the art of keyword research, identify your target audience's language, and weave these golden threads through your content, titles, and meta descriptions. Remember, relevance and intent are key; the right keywords attract the right customers, paving the way for successful conversions.

CONTENT: THE TAPESTRY OF ENGAGEMENT:

Think of your website as a canvas; your content, the vibrant paints that bring it to life. Craft compelling product descriptions, engaging blog posts, and informative guides that not only provide value but also resonate with your audience. Optimize your content for both users and search engines, incorporating natural language and rich imagery to weave a tapestry of engagement that keeps visitors enthralled and clicking "Buy Now."

Technical Optimization: The Hidden Looms:

While unseen, the technical aspects of your website are the sturdy looms upon which your SEO tapestry is woven. Ensure fast loading times, a mobile-friendly interface, and a clean website structure. Implement schema markup to provide rich data to search engines, and prioritize internal linking to guide users and bots alike through your virtual aisles. Remember, a technically sound website is a foundation for success, ensuring a seamless user experience and boosting your visibility in the eyes of search engines.

USER EXPERIENCE: THE ENCHANTED THREADS:

Your website is not just a digital marketplace; it's a haven for customer interaction. Prioritize user experience at every turn. Provide intuitive navigation, streamline checkout processes, and personalize the journey for each visitor. Enchant your website with user-friendly elements, interactive features, and engaging visuals, weaving a tapestry of experience that keeps customers coming back for more.

MOBILE OPTIMIZATION:
THE MICRO KINGDOM:

In today's digital world, the "micro kingdom" of mobile reigns supreme. Optimize your website for smaller screens, prioritize responsive design, and ensure a seamless shopping experience on smartphones and tablets. Remember, ignoring mobile optimization is like closing your doors to a vast majority of potential customers. Embrace the micro kingdom, and watch your sales soar as you cater to the ever-growing mobile audience.

CUSTOMER REVIEWS AND RATINGS: THE THREADS OF TRUST:

Social proof is a powerful currency in the online world. Encourage and manage customer reviews and ratings, showcasing them prominently on your website. Respond to both positive and negative feedback with grace and professionalism, weaving a tapestry of trust that attracts new customers and strengthens your brand image.

SITE SPEED: THE SWIFT SHUTTLE:

In the bustling marketplace of the internet, patience is a rare commodity. Ensure your website loads lightning-fast, optimizing images, minimizing HTTP requests, and leveraging caching mechanisms. Remember, a swift website is not just a perk; it's a fundamental pillar of e-commerce success, minimizing bounce rates and driving conversions.

E-COMMERCE SEO AND SOCIAL MEDIA INTEGRATION: THE INTERTWINED WEB:

Your website and social media are not isolated islands; they are threads woven into a single web of visibility. Share optimized content on social platforms, leverage influencers, and engage with your audience in real-time. Remember, the synergy between e-commerce SEO and social media amplifies your reach, builds brand awareness, and attracts a throng of loyal customers.

HANDLING OUT-OF-STOCK PRODUCTS: THE EMPTY ROOMS:

Out-of-stock products can pose challenges, but with proactive strategies, you can navigate these temporary setbacks. Be transparent, provide estimated restock dates, and offer similar product recommendations. Embrace pre-orders for highly anticipated items, and update out-of-stock pages to maintain relevance for future searches. Remember, out-of-stock situations are not roadblocks, but opportunities to engage with customers and build anticipation for future sales.

E-COMMERCE SEO ANALYTICS: THE GUIDING COMPASS:

Track and analyze key metrics like organic traffic, keyword rankings, and conversion rates. Utilize powerful tools like Google Search Console, SEMrush, and Ahrefs to gain valuable insights into your website's performance. Remember, SEO analytics is not a one-time treasure hunt; it's an ongoing journey of discovery and refinement.
**Staying Updated with SEO Trends: Chasing the Horizon

FAQS

1. "How often should I update my product titles and descriptions for SEO purposes?"

Regularly revisit your product titles and descriptions to ensure they remain relevant and reflect current SEO best practices. Quarterly reviews are a good target, allowing you to adjust for keyword trends, competitor changes, and evolving customer needs. Optimize titles with relevant keywords and concise clarity, while descriptions should be informative, engaging, and rich in detail to persuade and convert.

2. "Do social media signals directly impact search rankings?"

While social media signals like shares and mentions don't directly influence search rankings, they play a significant role in boosting your overall online visibility and driving traffic to your website. This increased traffic, engagement, and brand awareness can indirectly influence search algorithm factors like user dwell time and bounce rate, potentially contributing to positive ranking shifts over time.

3. "What tools are recommended for tracking e-commerce SEO analytics?"

Several powerful tools can help you monitor and analyze your e-commerce SEO performance. Some popular options include:

- Google Analytics: Provides an expansive overview of website traffic, user behavior, and conversion data.
- SEMrush: Offers in-depth analysis of keyword rankings, competitor research, and backlink monitoring.
- Moz: Focuses on technical SEO audits, keyword research, and on-page optimization insights.

Choosing the right tool depends on your specific needs and budget. Consider trying out free trials and comparing features before investing in a paid subscription.

4. "Can structured data markup be applied to any e-commerce platform?"

Structured data markup enhances how your website appears in search results by providing rich data about your products and content. Fortunately, you can implement structured data markup on most major e-commerce platforms. Consult your platform's documentation or support resources for specific instructions on adding schema markup to your product pages and website.

5. "Is mobile optimization essential for small e-commerce businesses?"

In today's mobile-first world, optimizing your website for mobile devices is absolutely essential for any e-commerce business, regardless of size. With the majority of online searches and purchases happening on smartphones and tablets, neglecting mobile optimization will significantly handicap your reach and potential conversions. Ensure your website is responsive, with easy navigation and clear visuals optimized for smaller screens.

Remember, mobile optimization is no longer an optional luxury; it's a fundamental requirement for success in today's e-commerce landscape. Make it a priority for your small business and watch your mobile sales and customer satisfaction soar.

THE END

ABOUT THE AUTHOR

Neil J Milliner

Neil J. Milliner is a contemporary author, creative educator, and publisher focusing on helping creatives, introverts, and musicians build authentic brands, overcome perfectionism, and navigate career challenges through practical, psychology-backed guides. He writes books on music marketing (*The Musician's Marketing Playbook), songwriting (*Emotional Hooks Handbook), sustainable living, self-improvement (*How to Feel Better Without Fixing Everything), and building creative spaces. He runs his own imprint, Books by Neil J, and emphasizes connecting with one's core self for aligned, meaningful creation.

Key Themes in His Work:
- Authenticity: Building brands and creating music that reflects your true self.
- Overcoming Perfectionism: Practical strategies to move past creative blocks and endless tweaking.
- Music Industry Guidance: Marketing, songwriting, and technical advice for musicians.
- Mindful Living: Eco-habits and personal growth for creatives.

Who He Helps:
- Musicians, songwriters, producers
- Creative introverts
- Entrepreneurs and creatives seeking genuine connection
- Individuals wanting to live more sustainably

www.ingramcontent.com/pod-product-compliance
Lightning Source LLC
Chambersburg PA
CBHW080957290526
45795CB00009B/2982